wild horses

wild horses

rob mclennan

The University of Alberta Press

Published by

The University of Alberta Press
Ring House 2
Edmonton, Alberta, Canada T6G 2E1

Library and Archives Canada Cataloguing in Publication

McLennan, Rob, 1970-
Wild horses / rob mclennan.

(CuRRents)
Poems.
ISBN 978-0-88864-535-7

I. Title. II. Series: Currents (Edmonton, Alta.)

PS8575.L4586W54 2010 C811'.54 C2009-906595-9

First edition, first printing, 2010.
Printed and bound in Canada by Houghton Boston Printers, Saskatoon, Saskatchewan.
Copyediting by Andy Weaver.

A volume in (*cuRRents*), a Canadian literature series.
Jonathan Hart, series editor.

The University of Alberta Press is committed to protecting our natural environment. As part of our efforts, this book is printed on Enviro Paper: it contains 100% post-consumer recycled fibres and is acid- and chlorine-free.

The University of Alberta Press gratefully acknowledges the support received for its publishing program from The Canada Council for the Arts. The University of Alberta Press also gratefully acknowledges the financial support of the Government of Canada through the Book Publishing Industry Development Program (BPIDP) and from the Alberta Foundation for the Arts for its publishing activities.

for Lainna,

There's a hand that thanks, that lies inside, that lines the hand that moves

—Cole Swensen, *the book of a hundred hands*

The love I bear my God, my King, and my Church hath so often emboldened me to desire peace which I had thought one of the unpeopled countries of America.

—Rosemary Waldrop, *shorter american memory*

they've heard that from the Edmonton International
you can see the curve of the earth.

—Erin Knight

contents

map of edmonton

a short walk into exile

> A fish swims through water, but is not
> of it.
>
> —Eric Paul Schaffer

a bowl you would be bullwhip.
into waves, a camisole canola foal

stickless; states an email jokes
into position of a final harvest

you would weather me when

an opening up of transfer, west; a soil
foreign; you shoulder

birds, upon

those are some heels; so might as well
cant find a glass

mostly, jacob; ladder into stars
& cloud

the bible belt suspends

perennial about; drink in me pear juice,
fermented, restless

no birds would suffer

I am not long, my self-imposed; if I am twinned,
or restless gone

if this my paris, new new york

what more you, skin?

at the edge of prairie there are no secrets

alberta notebooks:

this is not a line but line as
an artery repeats itself

the river bend & maybe curves
a ways into collusion

the steep end of the incline, rise; the wind
steam up

when they were most called alien,
they recognized in flesh

the colour of the beer is not the issue

a standard, of bearing down
or whistling

the pillow, a tiny
question

the yellow firetruck; a blues on whyte,
a tiny parce of land

spare change

the point of view begins to shift because

we are as permanent as meat; a rescue-toss

deploring down the main

power plant

a six month song; we may
have made a mistake

the choral leaf depends upon

a population turns the corner, turns
their head

strathcona down a notch & tired,
tired

hair of the dog

as quarters; 1800 portrait of a brood
of buckskin guns

goes history; justin timberlake
w/ wooden teeth

a frontier lonely

as a cloud; of horsehair,
keeping plaster cast

a championship

of black dogs & whirling,
insisting then to some

eleven lines of itchy sorrow

(after sharon thesen

could a lyric discontinue
after such abrasive terms

I hold you up

a moment after this
a moment after, thus

at the wrong end
of a minimum

one drink, & then
another

thousands of miles away
the fate of my right hand

the hills (the northern lights)

the ridge a rebel cleft, a music
in the works

or what does that mean

going under

arctic light a shifting simile, like sand
, road gravel ends of dirt

what you can almost see

rear window

a solipsism
of certain words

a campus wound

what do you know
, would a finger place

a vision
of seed

light brusque through the trees

water pumps stone,
circumnavigate rock

& then twists,
tinkles darker,

down

prose, a novel

if you so a month, a month
a tree-source disgorge words

a tone, a space, a rhythmic pattern
, it is a matter of power

what is shared in a particular

sure desire, didn't end up being
, the deep habits of classicism

no one in our community dared

through bawdy culture, sometimes
I would wake up & know

like clearing the bush, like all the lessons
cleared out in pieces

bleeding cannot be subjective

in the present tense, the one that sounds
, sometimes

I would wake up & know
a different version

in the person, second

after having spent so much time indoors

the space is bigger, after all; the office
where I spend & make my,

daily

a wall of thistles speckled flat

marked mid along the grain; canola
yellow talking soft

tween cellphones

every morning skip of soft white pages
slip

poem that echoes an earlier poem

the lake she swims
is only blue

filled w/ holes

in such a state

how many instances a lemon
or an orange

swollen on a branch
of never-seen

envy furls
& unfurls

madrigal for john & jean

> Now I know how it is
> with a cup to the ear of thunder
> —Kaia Sand, *interval*

a thirst made first
from a room & then
a house

w/ many windows

every thing & every
place
where they meet, a
still

distinction

or the market would turn
or the pool where she swam
but a girl

but the yet of woman

water goes down clear the ravine
& picks clean houses
fresh

out of history
out of strathcona ash

where an inverted mountain
ruptures

oil
& trestles

in the undertow
of rhythm & bees

& a train whistle north
neverends

the window of walls at the top of the world

in green directions, three
& a tilt

& a blazing design

in a town where everything
rises, eventually

spreads

the slow lava of houses
& building developed

metal cranes twin the eastern horizon

on the edge of prairie there are no secrets

the edge of this
, a gradient of means

holds
& further

the poem is north
& the rest

to tall tales,
love

, breakable
as skin

for scars, & a story
a steady frost of grain

assembles,
wood

a footfall hurricane
& the sideways draft

& if all the rest is dross

And all because it shines in the dark.
—Cole Swensen, *Goest*

a small sums of insecurity, & loss

a wave of designating fact & some familiars

discerning, if at all

why, if the sky more crisp

why, if leave the leafy trees come autumn

described, as evidenced by things

between them is immense

I would recall; a critical of coin & breath

an opening of the plains

closes a door
& a door

how do you solve a problem
like medea

a mountain
what youve never seen

john goodman
in barton fink

the pixies
, saskatoon

that one time

you said it
you said it,

again

the air
is thick enough

w/ dust

to be afraid
of venus flytraps

lost in translation

, what is

a pasteurized groan
through the everglades

where
you would buffalo

turn

, is

hesitation
& a house

that doesnt think

diffused light
on senses

dulled

a meaner end
, a means

,

it speaks
& speaks & then dis

solves

my life as a dead north-west explorer

(for paige ackerson-kiely

Plunder what is known.
—Nathalie Stephens, *Touch To Affliction*

Enough to say mind your beauty. Pallor. Blush.
Doesn't mean you're off scot-free. Start at the apple
and sweep upward toward your hairline.
—Sarah Lang, *The Work of Days*

the heart is no pervue; an astrolabe,
stardust

& deep;

if the mummified tale
of the permafrost lost; through

a capacity to hold, hold
, reduce; the west

instead of mutable

we adapt, they say; or do we
it is the only thing they tell

—

of a tell, a single mark
to give it away

we erode what we then never could

the fallacy of control, & of boundaries,
we live in the soil

I am line in the sand

I am the white man,
bringing smallpox in blankets & jars,

until its too late

athabasca, is

a legendary construct

a basin filled w/ holes

a ruperts land; a measure

a sextant nudge

a perpendicular landing

resident upon the river

a land of certain-born & stricken-white

the north saskatchewan

sternwheel & scow

a presence of missions & post

a boom young peace river trail

the south end of the trail, a landing

the last white stationary finger, pointed

a body of short memory
, of no consequence

if love would bear a god
of those first settlements

would bull a rifle butt
for buffalo thunder

would roar across
as earthquake wave

the wind that you yourself would blame

the sun thats been against us
, weeks

the line that david thompson four days lost
no longer knowing 49th

if he was north or south
of parallel

—

if born into a sulfuric country
a wild blackfly bleed

not where I originally

a loyal scotland
breach & body-torn

home again, you cant

, some thousand leagues

& when we die, recorded
w/ a stone

if the weather of hangmen
an uncommon charge

riding horses
from the mouth of the stain

a legislative bleed
across barrens

what the short grass & short legs
, an undertow

I am peopled the spirits
of simple ancestry

from king lear to cattle,
as wild as beasts

would you know yet to run,
cordelia

would you know yet to run
or as simple a thing

as come in from the rain

at the soul of the boat,

ice, as opposed
to the apparition of ice

where the water atones

maybe tomorrow, even

I am sorry

pastured green

& a healthy brown,
even black

not this trestle of faith
on this faithless blank

a mixture of exile
& days to adjust

a vague national anthem
we tried to forget

kind of freedom

—

a thorn in the marsh; if so
, beholden

history regenerates, doesn't even notice
it repeats

see, see, see; it runs
& it runs all over

a nail in a casket; driven down

where are you, bees?

my mouth horsehair dry
from speaking alphabet too many times

in the wrong order

my mouth is bone dry
working down to bare bone; strips of leather

once knew flesh, but has forgot

—

the word is a blossom; I am buried
at longitude, head down

so when I stand again I am pitch pointed north

wild horses

Every now & then
I feel you ignore me

Knee-deep in lust
    —Rod Smith, *Deed*

rereading paige ackerson-kiely on the airplane back to edmonton

if this delay were darkness,
it would never dawn. a series of delays,

which in the end, make up
a single wait.

a star would not abandon.

air & dust combine into immediate creation:
a baby, a magazine, plastic tumbler of gin.

books become unreadable; small bricks.

my whole life on this solid earth
& four hours more, the ground

become unbearable.

I was not looking at her fingers,
but I know where they were.

all the beautiful things might move.

'the girl from abbotsford'

the skin could be singed
from my toes to my tips

& would never still know

when your body unfolds
& unfolds, like a bare

piece of transparent tape

am rendered, I thus
I am sending a map

made of popsickle sticks

I am heavy; atlas
& have fallen through days

a service economy of sounds
& fake clouds

all the way from the kootenays

I am holding your taste
on my tongue like a verb

wild horses

she, says get a horse & go out
where the foothills

if any else sunlight in, given

by the side an hour lost, the blue
shifting sands of the northern lights

if spirited, to speak at a time
across one hundred & fourtieth

twenty minute north where need
& in the wrong

direction

poem for west edmonton mall

four phases; play, shop, stay, plan

the premiere piece of thus; a fishers ice

caught between its currency; of boundaries

located in edmonton, w/ these additions,
facts & statistics

a roller coaster overload come mirror lights
& whistle flash

a colour coded establishment; bodies drop
amusements pace

the replicated soul; *santa maria*

raising top from plastic; wooden birth

or façade down the boulevard

bombay sapphire gin, the taste
, colonial

what you cant together reach

a slip of bill

poem listening to my daughter at a distance of some thousand miles

> From the five good emperors
> I have learned that there were five good emperors.
> —Lisa Jarnot

the first casualty of travel
the sweep it creates

& sometimes provides

the wind out a breath
we would otherwise make

ontario snow up a wind chill
of alberta depth, some minus fifty

in your eighteenth year, a measure
, a bootstrap

you would yourself pull

a word from childhood
to measure: bare miles

a possible film treatment for the rest of the afternoon

> There is / no sense to beauty.
> — Ed Dorn

to ask 'winning aint anything'
but to her & to her & to him

neil young may be loud, but they
have a remote

what else drink suggested

& the lights all behind

the pull,
& the pull

of her fine boots & her
fine legs, poured

in the dark
& then into the dark

from whence they came

the ringing goes deeper
, deep

sex at thirty-eight

I'm calmer now, to learn. love may not save us.
—Barry McKinnon, "Sex at 38"

is less direct;

is not a boundary
or a given room, intact

& pushes, sometimes; strong

has nothing to prove
& everything

to suggest

is not where you are
or where you have

been

2.

restful, restless
all the same

is memory as much
as most

ten-fold, patience
, the sake of a wound

there is no what
there is no why

a math of sex
at thirty-eight

there is little
else

her simmerd smile
, laugh

After Spicer

There is a mind beating in that pile of rubble you call your
mind.
It occasionally astonished me.
—Jack Spicer, "Three Poems for Tish"

You are going south looking for a drinking fountain
I am going north looking for the source of the chill in my bones
—Jack Spicer, "Seven Poems for The Vancouver Festival"

—

a seriality, then remark
upon both houses

trading in a mud lark
spinning wheels a *transmit*

sense a swallow whispers

—

when talking mars a circuitry
of tangled matter
dictation

& its baseball law

; the serial function takes
a map
, a perpetual pattern

sustain a rhythm & then; televised coding

—

you don't get to catch
between his lines ; the ball

, or superimposed

monastic & in some, abstract

runcible mtn & what vital justice

, textbook of jeffers, or thirteen ways

of pitching past an orange

—

you might be putting voice
or distraction
; terms of,
or when limited to

a baroque never fixed

; when twenty-four

the act a pivotal question; afterlife

of mothers shoes

—

a hardly vocal   ; stays the same

            germanic house; the lone boy
in the lonesome bay

                        the intrigue of invisible

; or would emerge (his many questioned) dead

—

a dance, dictation
                                    misplacing politic
            against a taste for being

yearns   ;   the game a ball
                                    & ball game

; notions of a poet
or of an orange, sweeter

                        in the glove

—

                    the holy spark
of radio energy
                                ; hums
a turbulent lecture

to process ground experience; non-tragic math

          when tallman splinter,
a ghost-text of community

                    out upon; his poems
                              therefore speak

—

          a template of readership
                                , extolling virtues
of a special craft
                                          ; does thus,
where then are great

interfered; an accident w/ history
begins w/ announcements

a babel, in; a glass
of ultimately crucial

—

carted breath   ; before the horse

observance; essentially *think*, I thing

or terror-held degrees

                    ; a 1950s fortune
packed in palindrome

—

        divided by a big dark,
logos   ; an obscufated
        shadow

lets try the last; selection of,

        impossible to lowghost, the
                long-disappointed dog

inventing california, boston, faulkner

—

did you know;   as far as the strip
                                   & grail
        more magazines, will

would pay you through religion, stretch
                a future-self

to justify its own; awayside, mountain high
& through composed
                                        , a to the same
        , a letter

nevertheless; a publicly, discussed

—

denounce   marking, making
                screwed up

        , & they found; the human
counterpart of trees

        , a subway hand, the cruelty
                                   of moon,
                your ocean

the spartan twelve years old a fact

map of edmonton

for/after erin mouré

If I keep walking west
I can precede this time again
—Fanny Howe, *The Lyrics*

map of edmonton (prelude)

a touch
out of barren sympathies

you cant step into
the same river twice, you cant

go home again, they say

a stranger
in a strange van

a map of the mists
that came up off the floodgates

the green river snakes

does any traveller risk
becoming foreign to those

in his own lands?
his own?

map of edmonton (rossdale flats)

1.

a thin blue line, eight thousand
itinerant turns

of the sun featured earth

spark, a long heat of fiction

it's not a discovery
if they knew

drunk, cross
the high level bridge

festooned in air

vacant lot between building
& dance club

we dance, & we dance

just cause we have to

more than we want

2.

a kiss before something,
just leaving the car

a sweep, idle hand

a poem we make
out of printers ink,

accident

silver ribs
, river valley again

belgravia hearts

a kinetics of history
& polyglot glut

, maybe boxed

3.

under ten thousand wheels

the black dog burns
& then howls

a fingernail moon

this is north, sure
but not all the way

a signature, leaves

a poem, a napkin

a saint cannot sign

4.

the difference in depth
between angel

& river, pure
then & again

shall I say that all love

shall I say
that all blood

this is not
the ocean

5.

what does a map do
but place

all else; you know
where you were

when you started

a stamp, a fissure
taking hold

the car a small blue

a small stone
in the boot

pushing under

map of edmonton (garneau)

for andrea bloom

1.

, loss of soft flesh

a stretch of river-side

the night before

you turn & roses
turn

2.

conflicting songs
of televised debate

who
& then who

& a light
that just never

3.

a tremble of buildings
& the drunks pulling stools

would newly establish

a degree of what chemical
, makes

the scent of a wonder

amid melting snow
& the mud

the wind takes

map of edmonton (mill creek)

for christine stewart

1.

a site
& an order

, a line

the cross
& that

an even
loss

or
, what you

if cut
into low squalor

, day
& a dollar

2.

metal rust & money
, a tyrant of steel

the street breath
of children

plant line
of regal trees

a cartwheels
grassy gloss

& red purple light
, green

3.

a hesitate math
overwrit

can catch you at flags

did you list
at low end

or high

the mill creek bridge

is this tree
or tree-worth

I would anchor out

, sleep

map of edmonton (saskatchewan drive)

for andy weaver

1.

a river that would snake
a road

as simple as it could

, who else

would down upon,
a balcony

dont let the poem
end

or deep to burn

2.

he asks the crow,
instead

the magpie
lyric

& staccato
hop

3.

how green the cut
of valley deep

would enter, us
& them

when you were here
& here

the worst of sake

goes suffering
into

an oily flame

4.

this is spun out a curve
on the last turn of rock

on the line, on the breath

held down there by some

is this attention, or length
that compels

out the river

out the endless drive

map of edmonton (belgravia)

for doug barbour

1.

where trestle
comes up against bone

an endless spark, a promise

dont compete
for the same word

the ground relents
& the street goes

& the rock
& the stone

& the slapdash of houses
festooned

in postwar arc

2.

if you cut every sentence
like silk

or like leaves

in his basement office

in belgravia, nights
& the virginal self

& the olive, the olive

in new home

map of edmonton (birthday)

for myself, naturally

> the deal is this
> normal arc
>
> potatoes
> under the frozen earth
> — Fred Wah, *Articulations*

1.

a crossword our bodies
push into

of highways

a lie or a line

asks, how old are you now

a question
or statement

, reflection of birds
like an echo

, teamwork, no legs

a dream
to get nowhere

2.

a capture of dark
creeping up

these long years

never feel so, a maul
out of stone

& shopping

concentration
of birds

& belgravia, hearts
in a deadlock

, stone maul

3.

a slight, & a hope
out of sight

year is
year

, is

water, a genesis
of words

go speak ripe

am a portion of fish
winding trees

the accident is what
we had

in common

4.

where would I talk
that I still not get lost

in looking back

edmonton downs
& thus capital

cross across

neglected love
& wee bairn

or ghost of this place
, in caretakers grid

5.

does the day
earn the scope

of the pattern
, a thickness

of ages

I know not
what

when proved

to contradict
self

map of edmonton (windsor park)

for sheila watson

1.

a speed once achieved
you can never go back

, a corner of earth

brief throw
of what pebble or stone

could then slip across

the groat & that emily,
ms. murphy

, you steeped

it was not for the fish
put her hand in that river

2.

a signal of flesh
, bone

her big yellow coat

the victories little, he said
, but little enough

the cold, my darling,
so bitter, so dry

3.

at the end of the street
is a sign

at the end of the path

at the end of the day
it is melting through air

at the end of the pack
, a prayer

opens, a twist on words

at the end of the landing
the end of the porch

at the end of the book
she was from the beginning

map of edmonton (allandale)

for susanne luhmann & nat hurley

1.

do you know
where you are

if, as you said
in one fine place

at, finally,
one time

a suite
of three floors

paying for something
in return

try to figure out
what

in a surprising
lack

of rhyme

2.

not by a nose
or an even hair

a furtive
of depth

or a glance

or a basement
suiter than most

do you know
where you are

3.

if I have ever been visible
in light

slip
in the dark

too north
for the afternoon

turned into ever

do you know
where you are, where

you even have

the walls here
are thin

& the walls

every word
passes

a draft

map of edmonton (airport)

for lainna el jabi

if these floors
were transparent

an hour from town

would this cut
to the chaste

is when
not a when

but leduc

is not roof
but the rafters

map of edmonton (michaels park)

for catherine owen

1.

both times we arrived
we got lost in the same

& turned way all around

an archive
of light

& power, metal
spiked through the floor

in black
& back acreage

brings
a wet scratch

2.

simple, then
is a tightrope

fingers hushed

if this becomes
opposite

the bone
& the bleary gaze

, figured

3.

galvanized
across strings

one less
make eleven

, disharmony

speaking dischord,
a figure of speech

& cover-alls, bobcaygeon
a clawhammer

a statement of pine

a slap
on the thick wrist

of knowing

4.

is exile,
exactly

what
daylight

a sharp
glass

5.

the paddle
of sheep speech

on a beach
on an island,

where

above the iceline
, above mountains

& clouds

through the surface

I feel, what, tonight
& tomorrow

the sheer wish
of suburban

, a breath

of defiance

map of edmonton (rossdale)

for heather haley & devonia

1.

the halloween candy
of her best suit

a childhood version
of a knife

& then those heels

the picture
was never clear

somewhat vaguely
& said

if werent
& were are

2.

dawn, it
then blank

& cosmology
of known

were you midnight
at punk music

& a jar

water, out then
to the point

of absolute
& little maelstroms

acknowledgements

Some of these pieces have appeared, some in slightly altered forms, as various above/ground press broadsides, and in the journals *The Garneau Review* (Edmonton, AB/Ottawa, ON), Garry T. Morse's *Lexican Radio* (Vancouver, BC), Jennifer LoveGrove's *Dig* (Toronto, ON), *Interim* (Las Vegas, NV), *Nōd* (Calgary, AB), *Ottawa Arts Review* (Ottawa, ON), various issues of *The Peter F. Yacht Club* (Edmonton, AB/Ottawa, ON), on Blaine Greenwood's "Not Your Mother's Poetry," CKXU, 88.3 (Lethbridge, AB), on Ariel Gordon's May Day Poems blog during the month of May 2008 (*maydaypoems.blogspot.com*, Winnipeg, MB), the *Other Voices International* website (CA), the *Parliamentary Poet Laureate "Poem of the Week"* website, June 2008 (Ottawa, ON), as a feature on Anny Ballardini's *Poet's Corner — Fieralingue* website, and the author's own blog (*robmclennan.blogspot.com*). Earlier versions of some of the sections have also appeared as the chapbooks *After Spicer (draft)* (Ottawa, ON: Apostrophe Press, 2007) and *map of edmonton (rossdale flats)* (Ottawa, ON: above/ground press, 2008) and in *Alberta Dispatch: interviews and writing from Edmonton* (Ottawa, ON: above/ground press, 2008).

"madrigal for john and jean" is for John Worton and Jean McBean; "& if all the rest is dross" is for Cara Hedley; "an opening of the plains" outright *steals* a line from Guy Maddin (but only a little one); "lost in translation" is for Sarah Lang; "'the girl from abbotsford'" borrows its title from a line George McWhirter borrowed from somewhere else; "edmonton, alberta, september 22, 2007" knows who it's for; "wild horses" is for Nadine McInnis.

Thanks to Rhonda Douglas, who gave me the notebooks this book first took shape in; to Hudson's on Whyte, where this originally got started (during those first heady weeks), and the Garneau Pub on 109th & its various staff (special thanks to Andrea Bloom) where the bulk of this was eventually continued, completed.

Thanks to my Edmonton pals, including Trisia Eddy, Lainna El Jabi, Thomas Wharton, Christine Stewart, Jeff Carpenter, Catherine Owen, Alice Major, Shane at RATT, Shawna Lemay, Douglas Barbour and Michael Luski for their time, conversation and their ideas, both good and bad, some of which I have even followed. As well, thanks to Catherine, Trisia, Lainna and Sandra Ridley for editorial input, suggestions; thanks to Andy Weaver for a thorough and thoughtful edit, and everyone at University of Alberta Press for their help in seeing this project through. You have all helped make this a better book.

September 2007—May 2008
Edmonton, AB